A LOOK AT MONEY MATTERS

CURRENCY

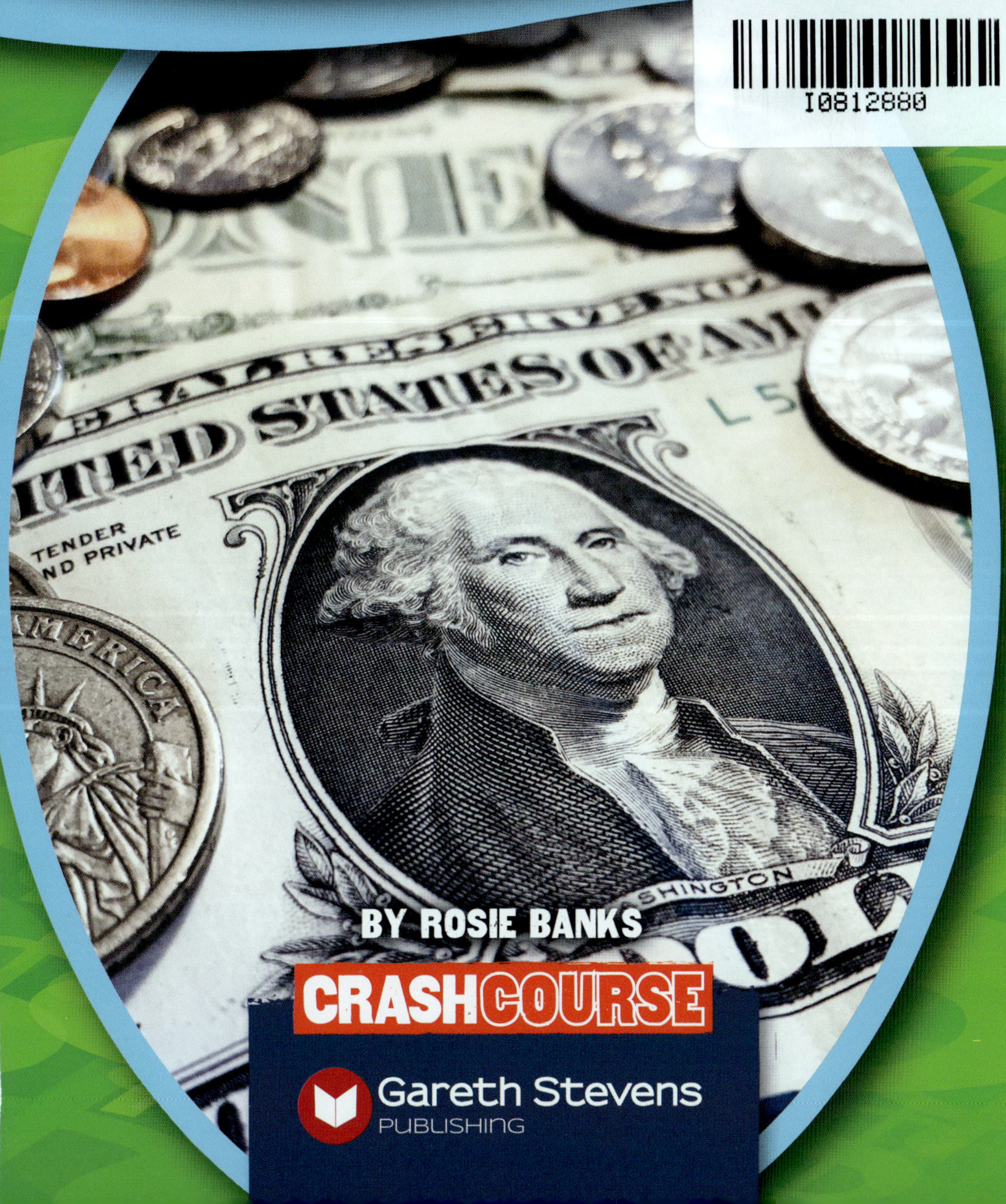

BY ROSIE BANKS

CRASHCOURSE

Gareth Stevens
PUBLISHING

Please visit our website, www.garethstevens.com. For a free color catalog of all our high-quality books, call toll free 1-800-542-2595 or fax 1-877-542-2596.

Library of Congress Cataloging-in-Publication Data
Names: Banks, Rosie, 1978- author.
Title: Currency / Rosie Banks.
Description: Buffalo : Gareth Stevens Publishing, [2024] | Series: A look at money matters | Includes index.
Identifiers: LCCN 2023025821 (print) | LCCN 2023025822 (ebook) | ISBN 9781538292280 (library binding) | ISBN 9781538292273 (paperback) | ISBN 9781538292297 (ebook)
Subjects: LCSH: Money--Juvenile literature.
Classification: LCC HG221.5 .B286 2024 (print) | LCC HG221.5 (ebook) | DDC 332.4--dc23/eng/20230626
LC record available at https://lccn.loc.gov/2023025821
LC ebook record available at https://lccn.loc.gov/2023025822

First Edition

Published in 2024 by
Gareth Stevens Publishing
2544 Clinton Street
Buffalo, NY 14224

Designer: Leslie Taylor
Editor: Therese Shea

Photo credits: Cover & Series Art (background) creativenv/Shutterstock.com; Series Art (falling coins) Abscent Vector/Shutterstock.com, (money photo) Giulio Benzin/Shutterstock.com; p. 5 Shawn Hempel/Shutterstock.com; p. 7 Roman Babakin/Shutterstock.com; p. 9 (background) Mltz/Shutterstock.com, (coins) CNG/https://en.wikipedia.org/wiki/File:Carthage_EL_shekel_2250013.jpg; p. 11 (building) Beyond My Ken/https://commons.wikimedia.org/wiki/File:United_States_Mint_Philadelphia.jpg, (coins) andrea crisante/Shutterstock.com; p. 13 vetkit/Shutterstock.com; p. 15 (10,000 bill) The Bureau of Engraving and Printing/https://commons.wikimedia.org/wiki/File:US-$10000-FRN-1934-Fr.2231-E.jpg, (fanned bills) Waxen/Shutterstock.com; p. 17 Bjoern Wylezich/Shutterstock.com; p. 19 Pedal to the Stock/Shutterstock.com; p. 21 alexkich/Shutterstock.com; p. 23 Vergani Fotografia/Shutterstock.com; p. 25 Oasishifi/Shutterstock.com; p. 27 PixieMe/Shutterstock.com; p. 29 rootstock/Shutterstock.com; p. 30 AdresiaStock/Shutterstock.com.

Printed in the United States of America

CPSIA compliance information: Batch #CW24GS: For further information contact Gareth Stevens at 1-800-542-2595.

CONTENTS

Currency Is Money....4
Bartering Was First....6
Creating Currency....8
Minting Money....10
Banknotes....14
Fiat Money....18
Name That Currency....20
The Exchange Rate....22
A New Look....24
Digital Currency....26
Circulation....28
More World Currency Names and Symbols....30
Glossary....31
For More Information....32
Index....32

Words in the glossary appear in **bold** type the first time they are used in the text.

CURRENCY IS MONEY

You know what money can do. It helps you buy goods and services. The money of a country is called its currency. Currency can be both **coins** and paper notes. Coins and notes represent, or stand for, different amounts of money.

MAKE THE GRADE

Money is called a medium of exchange. That just means it's something that can be traded for something else.

BARTERING WAS FIRST

Long ago, there was no currency. People traded what they had for what they needed. This is called bartering. For example, they might have traded animal furs for salt. People around the world still barter for the goods and services they need.

MAKE THE GRADE

People have been bartering for at least 8,000 years.

CREATING CURRENCY

People began using currency for the first time in **Mesopotamia** about 5,000 years ago. Other **civilizations** then made their own currency. Using currency is often easier than bartering. It's light to carry. It lasts a long time. People know its value too.

MAKE THE GRADE

Mesopotamian coins were called shekels.

MINTING MONEY

A mint is a place that makes coins. "To mint" means to make coins by stamping metal. The United States has four coin-making mints. They're in Philadelphia, Pennsylvania; Denver, Colorado; San Francisco, California; and West Point, New York.

MAKE THE GRADE

Today's U.S. coins are worth 1¢, 5¢, 10¢, 25¢, 50¢, and $1.

Mints use large machines to make coins from different metals. In the United States, coins are made of copper, zinc, and nickel. Pennies, dimes, and quarters are made of **layers** of metals. Nickels are made of mixed nickel and copper.

MAKE THE GRADE

You can see copper at the edge of quarters and dimes.

BANKNOTES

The U.S. Bureau of Engraving and Printing, or BEP, makes paper currency. These are called banknotes or bills. There are $1, $2, $5, $10, $20, $50, and $100 bills. The government discontinued, or took out of use, the $500, $1,000, $5,000, and $10,000 bills in 1969.

MAKE THE GRADE

U.S. banknotes are also called **Federal Reserve** notes.

U.S. banknotes aren't printed on paper from trees. Instead, they're made of **linen** and cotton. The BEP can print about 8,000 sheets of banknotes an hour. There are many pictures, colors, and numbers on each banknote. Printing money takes over 65 steps!

MAKE THE GRADE

Banknotes are printed on large sheets of paper. Then, they're cut into different bills.

FIAT MONEY

A dollar bill is just a piece of paper. A coin is a piece of metal. Their value comes from the government saying that they're legal tender. That means they must be taken as payment. Currency backed by governments is called fiat money.

MAKE THE GRADE

U.S. currency's value was once backed by gold. This was called a gold standard. One dollar was worth an amount of gold. No countries use the gold standard today.

NAME THAT CURRENCY

More than 200 currencies are in use today. Countries have different names for their currency. The United States and Canada call their currency the dollar. The currency used in the **European Union** is called the euro. Japan's currency is the yen.

MAKE THE GRADE

When many countries join the European Union, they adopt, or begin to use, the euro currency. Like the U.S. dollar, there are 100 cents in 1 euro.

THE EXCHANGE RATE

You can exchange, or trade, one country's currency for another country's currency. They often aren't equal. In July 2023, 1 U.S. dollar was worth 1.31 Canadian dollars. Currency exchange rates go up and down based on countries' **economies** and world events.

MAKE THE GRADE

Some countries accept other countries' currencies. For example, Zimbabwe takes U.S. money as legal tender.

A NEW LOOK

In the United States, new images, or pictures, on coins happen through a law made by Congress. Congress has honored states, national parks, U.S. women, and presidents with coins. The U.S. Department of Treasury has the final say over the images on banknotes.

MAKE THE GRADE

Some people collect old currency. U.S. half-cent coins stopped being made in 1857. Today, they can be worth hundreds of dollars—or more!

DIGITAL CURRENCY

Have you heard of Bitcoin or other **virtual** currencies? They're called cryptocurrencies. They aren't backed by a government. They're stored and exchanged as **digital** files. Some people don't trust cryptocurrencies. Their value can go up and down quickly. Others don't mind the **risks**.

MAKE THE GRADE

Cryptocurrency computers use a lot of energy, or power. If the Bitcoin currency were a country, it would use as much energy as the country of Argentina!

CIRCULATION

Banks remove notes from **circulation** when they aren't in good condition. U.S. 1 dollar banknotes last about six years. Other bills last longer. U.S. coins can last about 30 years. New currency goes to Federal Reserve banks and then to other banks for people's use.

MAKE THE GRADE

The Federal Reserve makes some old banknotes into **compost** for gardens!

MORE WORLD CURRENCY NAMES AND SYMBOLS

₿ Bitcoin	$ US . Dollar	£ UK . Pound	¥ China . Yuan	€ EU . Euro
₱ Cuba . Peso	₦ Nigeria . Naira	₡ Costa Rica . Colón	฿ Thailand . Bhat	₭ Laos . Kip
₩ Korea . Won	Rs Pakistan . Rupee	₴ Ukraine . Hryvna	¥ Japan . Yen	₽ Russia . Rouble
R$ Brazil . Real	A$ Australia . Dollar	J$ Jamaica . Dollar	Rp Indonesia . Rupiah	RM Malaysia . Ringgit
₺ Turkey . Lira	₫ Vietnam . Dong	C$ Canada . Dollar	₪ Israel . Shekel	KD Kuwait . Dinar
ريال Saudi Arabia . Riyal	₹ India . Rupee	Z$ Zimbabwe . Dollar	zł Poland . Zloty	kr Denmark . Krone

GLOSSARY

circulation: The state of being moved from place to place.

civilization: Organized society with written records and laws.

coin: A metal piece, often round and flat, released by a government as money.

compost: Matter made from rotten food, cut grass, and other materials. It's added to soil to make it better.

digital: Having to do with or using computers.

economy: The money made in an area and how it is made.

European Union: Also called the EU, a political and economic group of European countries.

Federal Reserve: The U.S. central banking system, which oversees the country's money supply as well as manages other financial duties.

layer: One thickness of something lying over or under another.

linen: A kind of cloth that is made from the stalks of the flax plant.

Mesopotamia: An area of Western Asia between the Tigris and Euphrates Rivers.

risk: The possibility of losing money.

virtual: Describing something that exists or happens on computers.

FOR MORE INFORMATION

BOOKS

Fitzpatrick, Kalpana. *Get to Know Money: A Fun Visual Guide to How Money Works and How to Manage It.* New York, NY: DK Publishing, 2022.

Gifford, Clive, and Rob Flowers. *A Quick History of Money: From Bartering to Bitcoin.* Beverly, MA: Wide Eyed Editions, 2021.

WEBSITE

U.S. Mint Classroom
www.usmint.gov/learn/kids/about-the-mint
The U.S. Mint offers interesting information about money and how it's made.

Publisher's note to educators and parents: Our editors have carefully reviewed these websites to ensure that they are suitable for students. Many websites change frequently, however, and we cannot guarantee that a site's future contents will continue to meet our high standards of quality and educational value. Be advised that students should be closely supervised whenever they access the internet.

INDEX

barter, 6, 7, 8
Bureau of Engraving and Printing (U.S.), 14, 16
coin, 4, 10, 11, 12, 13, 18, 24, 25, 28
cryptocurrency, 26, 27
exchange rate, 22
European Union, 20, 21
Federal Reserve, 15, 29
fiat money, 18, 19
Mesopotamia, 8, 9
mint, 10, 12
paper money, 4, 14, 15, 16, 17, 18, 24, 28, 29
Treasury Department (U.S.), 24